HOW WE CAN LIVE

HOW WE CAN LIVE

PRINCIPLES OF BLACK LIVES MATTER

Written by **Laleña Garcia**

Illustrated by **Caryn Davidson**

with the **Black Lives Matter Global Network Foundation**

Lee & Low Books Inc.
New York

To my family, for always making me laugh and feel loved.
And especially to my abuela, who spent her whole life
showing us all what it truly means to be unapologetic.
—L.G.

To Solei, Michael, Jasmaine, Phoebe, Naya, Brys, Jabiah, Umahani, Awa,
Jasmine, Bryanne, Julio, Matt, Max, Ari, Dania, Samiha, Elizabeth, and all of
my former and current students who inspire me and embody the true meaning
of these principles — who have shown their communities how we can live in
racially just and liberated ways.
—C.D.

LEE & LOW BOOKS Inc.
95 Madison Avenue
New York, NY 10016
leeandlow.com

Edited by Cheryl Klein
Book design by Rachel Eeva Wood with Caryn Davidson and Abhi Alwar
Production by the Kids at Our House
The text is set in Solway and the illustrations were rendered digitally.
Manufactured in China by RR Donnelley

10 9 8 7 6 5 4 3 2 1

First Edition

Cataloging-in-Publication data is on file with the Library of Congress.
ISBN 978-1-64379-496-9

A Note about the Text

As the Black Lives Matter principles are a living document, they have shifted in number and expression through the years. In early 2017, Tamara Anderson, a parent and activist in Philadelphia, distilled each principle from the Black Lives Matter website at that time into a one- or two-word phrase as a way to highlight the goals of the movement for her daughter. This language was subsequently adopted by the steering committee for Black Lives Matter at School, a national coalition advocating for racial justice in education, and I took inspiration from Tamara's phrases to translate the principles into kid-friendly language for classrooms. You can turn to the last page of this book to see the most recent statement of the organization's principles, and blacklivesmatteratschool.com/13-guiding-principles for the version I adapted for this book.

— **Laleña Garcia**

Illustrator's Note

Young people are often taught about Black history and social movements as being impacted and led by specific individuals, and they often only hear about the more popular and visible people, or those selected as symbolic icons of movements or time periods. The illustrations in this book feature historical leaders, contemporary activists, and other public figures, but they also include "everyday people" who are effective and active within their own communities and truly embody the meaning of these principles. All of these individuals have supported and uplifted Black lives in their work, in their activism, and in their own families and everyday lives — and this is the work (and reality) that makes a movement much more than the few names or icons associated with it.

— **Caryn Davidson**

WHAT IS BLACK LIVES MATTER?

Have you ever heard people say "Black Lives Matter"? Do you wonder what those words mean?

"Black Lives Matter" has become a powerful phrase all over the world because it is both a REMINDER and a PROMISE. It reminds us that, even today, Black people are treated differently because of the color of their skin — like their lives don't matter — and **that's not okay.** It reminds us that Black lives **should** matter, and that it's our responsibility to make a world that is safe and fair for everybody. When we say "Black Lives Matter," we are REMINDING ourselves and others that the world is still not fair, and we are PROMISING to work to **make** the world fair.

Black Lives Matter is also an organization and a civil rights movement founded by three Black women: Alicia Garza, Patrisse Cullors, and Ayọ Tometi (formerly known as Opal Tometi). You might have heard news stories where a white person killed a Black person and did not receive a punishment for it. In 2013, after something like this happened, Alicia poured her sadness and her ongoing faith in Black people into an internet post, declaring, "Black lives matter." Patrisse realized how important this idea was, so she shared it with lots and lots of people, and Ayọ figured out how to use the internet to tell even more people. Soon, many, many

ALICIA GARZA, PATRISSE CULLORS, and AYỌ TOMETI

people began using the words "Black Lives Matter" to talk about times when they saw that Black people were not being treated fairly. Alicia, Patrisse, and Ayọ then started an organization to support people who stand up for Black lives in many different ways. Anybody who cares about things being fair can be part of the Black Lives Matter movement.

Early in the life of their organization, the three founders, together with other activists, created a set of guiding principles. A principle isn't the person in charge of your school; that's a *principal*, which is spelled differently. A "principle" is an idea that you think is so important that you use it to help you make all your choices. For example, if you and your family have the principle that "Everyone is included," then when your little sibling asks if they can play with you and your friends, you might think about that principle as you decide how to respond. It might be hard to find a way to include your sibling in your game, but you know that it's something that is important for your family. You also know that other people in your family will include you in *their* games, and this principle makes your family stronger, more inclusive, and more fun.

Principles can also guide the rules we create together in our communities. Another example of a principle is "School is a place where kids and teachers have to be safe." If that's a principle in your school, then your classroom might have rules like "Be gentle with people's bodies" or "Take care of people's feelings." Those rules help everyone in the community follow the principle. Principles help us make decisions that we will feel good about, decisions that show us and the world who we want to be.

The principles in this book come from Alicia, Patrisse, and Ayọ's ideas about how they think the world could be. When we imagine the world we want to live in, we might think about people taking care of each other, sharing joy and curiosity and wonder, and celebrating all the members of their community—including people who don't always get the support they deserve, like elders, women, and queer and trans folks. We might imagine people having all the things they need to be happy and healthy and safe, like friends to play with and time to dream. Lots of times, when kids imagine the world they want, it looks a lot like the world Alicia, Patrisse, and Ayọ imagined.

Grown-ups sometimes think that big ideas like equity (making sure everyone gets what they need) and justice (making sure everything is fair) are too tricky for kids. But they're not! Sometimes kids actually have much better ideas about equity and justice than grown-ups, because grown-ups have gotten used to thinking about the world in the same old ways, and kids are good at finding new ways to think about the world. You can often do this just by asking questions about the things you see that aren't fair. One thing you might think about is how we build *systems* that help people.

"What are *systems*?" you might ask. Great question! Systems are the rules and practices we put in place to support the stories we tell about the world, and the ways we try to get other people to tell the same stories. You've heard some of these stories. A long time ago, some people told a story that said that people with lighter skin were better than people with darker skin. They kept telling this story until a lot of people believed it, and then it seemed okay to some people to enslave Black people. After slavery ended in the United States, it still seemed okay to many people to have systems that didn't let Black people vote (even though the law said they could), or go to the schools they wanted, or live where they wanted to live. You've probably already learned about people like Martin Luther King, Jr. and Rosa Parks. They worked with many, many other people to change the stories that were being told, and, slowly, some of the systems started to change too.

But systems are tricky, because they're almost invisible, and some of the systems that held up the old stories are still here. The principles of Black Lives Matter offer new stories for how we can live our lives. They show ways we can use new systems, like restorative justice and Black villages, instead of old systems, like the police and neighborhoods that make it hard for Black people to create community. Grown-ups right now all across the country are thinking about how to make new systems that support our new stories.

We need you to help grown-ups tell new stories—stories about a world where everyone is safe, has what they need, and can work together to make their community stronger. We need your help, because you have great imaginations, and you can imagine the world the way it **should** be. Grown-ups try, but our imaginations have gotten rusty. We've gotten used to the systems we have, and that makes it hard for us to think of ways to change them.

Friends, the most important thing you can do right now is to think up new systems for your new stories. Maybe in the world you imagine for us, everyone—kids and grown-ups together—can keep dreaming, hoping, and building a better life together. Please keep helping us.

UNAPOLOGETICALLY BLACK

Everyone should feel proud of who they are, and everyone should feel comfortable and confident standing up for what they believe. It's important to make sure that all people are treated fairly, and that's why we and millions of other people all over the country and the world are part of the Black Lives Matter movement. **We stand up for all Black lives to create a world where all Black people can be Unapologetically Black.**

WHAT DO YOU THINK IT MEANS TO BE UNAPOLOGETICALLY BLACK?

WHY WOULD SOMEONE FEEL LIKE THEY HAD TO APOLOGIZE FOR BEING BLACK?

HOW DO YOU IMAGINE IT WOULD FEEL TO LIVE IN A WORLD WHERE EVERYONE IS FREE TO BE THEMSELVES?

CHARLENE CARRUTHERS: Black, queer feminist community organizer; founding national director of BYP100; founder and executive director of the Chicago Center for Leadership and Transformation.

DIVERSITY

Even though there are many ways we are the same, we know that there are also ways we are different. When we get to hear ideas from lots of people, we get smarter; when we work together, our communities get stronger. It's important that we have lots of different kinds of people in our community and that everyone feels safe. When that happens, **our community shows its diversity.**

THINK ABOUT YOUR FRIENDS. WHAT ARE SOME OF THE WAYS YOU ARE DIFFERENT FROM THEM?

WHAT IS SOMETHING THAT YOU'VE LEARNED FROM THOSE DIFFERENCES?

Clockwise from bottom left: **SONIA GUIÑANSACA:** award-winning queer migrant poet, cultural organizer, and social justice activist · **JASILYN CHARGER:** Cheyenne River Sioux Land Defender and youth advocate for Native American and LGBTQ rights · **BAYARD RUSTIN** (1912-1985): Black, gay, Quaker civil rights activist who served as a Freedom Rider, a coordinator of the 1963 March on Washington for Jobs and Freedom, and a labor organizer promoting the desegregation of trade unions · **CIARA TAYLOR:** co-founder of the Dream Defenders, popular educator, grassroots organizer, and artist · **KAY ULANDAY BARRETT:** a pin@y-amerikan transgender disabled queer poet, performer, and educator.

EMPATHY

Different people have different feelings. It's our responsibility to take care of each other's feelings, so it can be helpful to think about how we would feel if something that happened to someone else happened to us. Even if we would react differently, understanding how another person feels is one way we can take care of each other in our community. When we understand and respect another person's feelings, **we are practicing empathy.**

THINK OF A TIME YOU NEEDED TO UNDERSTAND THE FEELINGS OF ANOTHER KID OR A GROWN-UP. WAS IT EASY, OR HARD, OR BOTH?

WHY DID YOU THINK IT WAS IMPORTANT TO USE EMPATHY?

HOW DID IT MAKE YOU FEEL?

WHAT DID YOU LEARN?

LOVING ENGAGEMENT

We want our communities to be places where all people feel seen, heard, and loved. To make this happen, we must always try to be fair and peaceful and treat other people with love. We have to keep practicing this in our communities so we can get better and better at it. When we do this, **we show loving engagement.**

THINK OF A TIME YOU WORKED HARD TO MAKE SURE YOU WERE FAIR AND PEACEFUL WITH ANOTHER PERSON. WHAT HELPED YOU BE ABLE TO KEEP PRACTICING JUSTICE AND PEACE?

THINK BACK TO A TIME WHEN YOU HAD A FIGHT WITH SOMEONE. WHAT WOULD IT HAVE LOOKED LIKE TO HAVE HAD A LOVING ENGAGEMENT INSTEAD?

RESTORATIVE JUSTICE

In our community, if someone causes a problem, they have to take responsibility for it; they can't just say "Sorry" and walk away. We know that when kids make mistakes, they should be allowed to make a better choice another time, and it's grown-ups' job to help them make better choices and give them other chances. We also know that when a person is able to fix a problem they've caused, this not only solves the problem, but it also helps the person who caused the problem more than a punishment would. When we try to heal the hurt on both sides, **we practice restorative justice.**

THINK OF A TIME YOU WORKED OUT A PROBLEM WITH ANOTHER PERSON. HOW DID YOU MAKE SURE EVERYONE WAS TAKEN CARE OF?

WHAT DID YOU LEARN FROM TALKING WITH THE OTHER PERSON AND LISTENING TO THEIR POINT OF VIEW?

BLACK FAMILIES

A family is a group of people who love and take care of one another. There are lots of different kinds of families, and we want to make sure that all families feel welcome in our community. **We support Black families.**

WHO ARE THE PEOPLE IN YOUR FAMILY?

WHAT IS DIFFERENT AND SPECIAL ABOUT EACH MEMBER OF YOUR FAMILY?

WHAT RESPONSIBILITIES DOES EACH PERSON IN YOUR FAMILY HAVE?

WHAT ARE SOME WAYS THE PEOPLE IN YOUR FAMILY TAKE CARE OF ONE ANOTHER?

INTER-
GENERATIONAL

It's important that we have spaces where people of different ages can come together, share their ideas, and learn from one another. When we do that, **it means our community is intergenerational.**

WHO ARE THE PEOPLE YOU CARE ABOUT AND LEARN FROM WHO ARE OLDER THAN YOU? YOUNGER THAN YOU?

WHAT IS SPECIAL TO YOU ABOUT GETTING TO SPEND TIME WITH PEOPLE WHO ARE NOT THE SAME AGE AS YOU?

BLACK VILLAGES

There are many ways to make a community. The people in a community might be related, or they might have chosen to become part of that community. Everyone in a community has a responsibility to take care of all the other members of that community. Another word for a community is a village. **We celebrate Black villages.**

WHO ARE THE PEOPLE AND FAMILIES
IN YOUR VILLAGE?

HOW DID THEY BECOME PART
OF YOUR VILLAGE?

BLACK WOMEN

We know that all people are important and have the right to be safe and talk about their feelings, even though some people might think that women and girls are less important than men and boys. **We stand with Black women.**

WHO ARE SOME BLACK WOMEN
OR GIRLS THAT YOU VALUE?

WHAT HAVE YOU LEARNED
FROM THEM?

HOW DO YOU SHOW THEM
YOU CARE ABOUT THEM?

Clockwise from top left: **KAHRIN BENNETT:** art educator, visual artist, writer, and warrior mom · **JUNE JORDAN** (1936–2002): Jamaican American and queer poet, teacher, and prominent figure in the Civil Rights, feminist, antiwar, and LGBTQ movements · **ASHNI SUNDER:** Body- and Soul-Centered therapist, facilitator, and human · **APRIL GURLEY:** social worker, motivational speaker, author, consultant, and educator · **DENISHA JONES:** teacher educator, critical scholar, true-play advocate, and Black Lives Matter at School steering committee member.

QUEER AFFIRMING

Everybody has the right to listen to their own heart and mind and choose how they describe themselves, who they love, and the kind of family they want. When we understand that people may love people of many different genders and we support them to make their own decisions, **we are queer affirming.**

WHO ARE SOME OF THE PEOPLE YOU LOVE?

WHY IS IT IMPORTANT FOR PEOPLE TO MAKE THEIR OWN DECISIONS ABOUT WHO THEY LOVE AND THE KIND OF FAMILY THEY WANT TO HAVE?

MALCOLM SHANKS: activist, political educator, and consultant; co-creator of the zine *Decolonizing Gender: A Curriculum*; former Senior Trainer at Race Forward and organizer at the National LGBTQ Task Force.

TRANSGENDER AFFIRMING

Everyone gets to listen to their own heart and mind to decide whether they are non-binary, a girl, or a boy, or if they want to use a different word to describe their gender. When a person is born, their grown-ups generally decide whether to call them a girl or a boy. Sometimes that decision doesn't match who the person really is, and that person is transgender. Sometimes that decision does match who the person really is, and that person is cisgender. When we work to make certain that all transgender people feel loved, safe, and seen, **we are being transgender affirming.**

HOW DO YOU FEEL WHEN SOMEONE ELSE TELLS YOU WHAT "GIRLS SHOULD DO" OR "BOYS SHOULD DO"?

HOW DO YOU THINK PEOPLE GOT THOSE IDEAS?

GLOBALISM

Black people live all over the world; some live in cities, some live in towns or villages, and some live in the countryside. When we think about all the different kinds of Black folks on the planet, and how their experiences are connected, even though they might be different, **we demonstrate globalism.**

WHAT DO YOU HOPE FOR BLACK CHILDREN AND FAMILIES AROUND THE WORLD?

WHAT QUESTIONS DO YOU HAVE FOR THEM?

RON DELLUMS (1935–2018): a self-described socialist and radical who served as US Representative from Oakland, California, from 1971 to 1998. He led House inquiries into US war crimes during the Vietnam War, sponsored successful legislation to end American investment in South Africa during the apartheid era, and fought to redirect military spending to housing, health care, and education.

COLLECTIVE VALUE

Everybody is important and has the right to be safe and happy, no matter what religion they are, how much money they have, where they come from, their abilities or disabilities, or who they love. There are so many different people in the world, but we love them all and fight for justice for them all. **We believe in our collective value, and the collective value of all Black people.**

WHAT ARE SOME THINGS YOU CAN DO IN YOUR EVERYDAY LIFE TO MAKE SURE THAT EVERYONE AROUND YOU FEELS LOVED, APPRECIATED, AND SAFE?

WHAT DO YOU NEED FROM YOUR COMMUNITY TO FEEL LOVED, APPRECIATED, AND SAFE?

Clockwise from left: **IANNE FIELDS STEWART:** Black, queer, and transfeminine founder of The Okra Project, a collective that seeks to address the global crisis faced by Black trans people • **ZAKIYAH ANSARI:** Black Muslim mom of eight and director of the New York State Alliance for Quality Education • **TAMARA ANDERSON:** educator, anti-racist trainer, artist, journalist, and organizer with the Black Lives Matter at School movement • **JESSE HAGOPIAN:** teacher, writer, and organizer with the Black Lives Matter at School movement.

AN AFTERWORD FOR ADULTS

In the summer of 2020, as the United States was dealing with a global pandemic, a Black man named George Floyd was murdered by a white police officer in Minneapolis. This reminder of systemic injustice and the need for Black Lives Matter brought people into the streets in unprecedented numbers. By the end of the summer, demonstrations and protests had taken place in over seventy countries, in the largest uprising against white supremacy the world had ever seen. The reverberations of that summer have continued as city councils vote to defund the police, school systems make arrangements to get cops out of schools, students across the country demand institutional accountability and change, and institutions and individuals do the messy work of grappling with the harmful narratives they've internalized.

While the original uprising was happening, I was teaching five- and six-year-olds over videoconference, a medium where children felt far less comfortable than they would have in my classroom. I received an email from a parent saying that their child wanted to talk to me about the Floyd murder, but also didn't want to scare their classmates. Our teaching team set up a meeting for the children and families who wanted to process and problem-solve together. While it was the hardest meeting I have ever run, it also planted a seed for this book, when a six-year-old asked, "How did all this even start?"

As I explained about systems and stories, it struck me that the very real confusion children feel when faced with systemic injustice is key to understanding how to change things. Children ask questions like, "But why doesn't everyone have a home?" or "Why wouldn't bosses pay their workers enough money to buy food?" or "Why weren't kids with different skin colors allowed to go to school together?" Finding honest answers to those questions often causes adults to feel uncomfortable, because they force us to fall back on the stories we've been told over and over, and those stories are not only harmful, they don't ring true to children ("Some people don't deserve a home? It's more important for the boss or company to make lots of money than for everyone to eat? People with different skin colors can't learn together?").

Eventually, kids hear the stories enough times that they internalize them as well. Hopefully that's where this book (and lots more like it!) comes in: We grown-ups can interrupt the harmful narratives that we've been told, and make sure that we **don't** pass them on to children. Instead, we can nurture their innate sense of justice and curiosity by encouraging them to ask questions, to practice compassion, to approach different situations with a sense of possibility. We can also be honest and vulnerable with them: "When I was a kid, no one talked about systems, so it's kind of new to me and I'm still learning. We can learn together." If you're committed to this work as well, read on for more ideas on having conversations about race with children.

*A*void thinking of this as a single conversation. As we speak to children about racism—or really, any kind of oppression—it's important that we avoid the trap of having a single conversation explaining oppression as an interpersonal situation. For example, "Racism is when a white person is unkind to a Black person" is overly simplistic and ignores structural and systemic racism. We need to have ongoing conversations with children, conversations that evolve as they mature. You wouldn't show a child a picture of the alphabet once or twice and assume that now they know how to read. It takes years! Learning anything takes years, and this particular kind of learning is constantly being undermined by the society we live in, which gives kids a thousand competing messages about race every day. By making race, power, and justice regular and comfortable topics of conversation, you'll enable your children to think critically and respond in healthy ways. If children point out inequity, encourage them to think about why it's happening and what they could do about it. Take them seriously, and see if you can try out any of their ideas, even small ones. When you offer children opportunities to act, you help them to realize that things can be changed, and that they can have a hand in making the world more fair.

Focus on the goals and principles of Black Lives Matter rather than deaths and violence. In order to create a better reality, this book, like the guiding principles themselves, deliberately concentrates on the strength and wisdom of Black people and communities rather than the fear and violence of white supremacy. Many children, especially older children, may be aware of police brutality toward Black people, and it's our responsibility to give them opportunities to share their experiences and questions in a safe space. It's important that we're honest with our young people, and acknowledge the reality of racialized violence. At the same time, focusing on the violence of white supremacy can be traumatizing to children, especially Black children. **Talking about the guiding principles instead offers a way to discuss these problems with an emphasis on hope and action.** The guiding principles provide a framework for a more just society, and young children have an innate sense of justice; I often see them nodding in agreement when I introduce a new principle. Linking the principles of Black Lives Matter to the ideas we use in our classrooms or families on a regular basis helps children understand the connections between justice and equity on a large scale and their own lives and individual actions.

Talk about systems and power. We also have a responsibility to explain the systems that have upheld racism in our country—Jim Crow, redlining, tying school funding to property values, the school-to-prison pipeline, etc.—so that children can understand what we're trying to change. Kids know all about power, and by naming it and pointing out examples of it in our everyday lives, you help children develop a critical lens through which to view the world, and, in turn, to change it. If you'd like a look at the language I use to explain systems to young children, check out the introduction. You can also find additional discussion questions, lesson plans, and other resources to use in conjunction with this book at leeandlow.com/books/how-we-can-live.

Spend *some time dreaming.* On the next page, you'll find the history and vision of the BLM movement, as beautifully expressed by Alicia Garza, Patrisse Cullors, Ayọ Tometi, and the organization they founded, the Black Lives Matter Global Network Foundation. As you consider their words, ask yourself: What might our society look like if we emphasized community and compassion rather than competition? Choose one aspect of their vision and imagine it playing out in a variety of scenarios: How might the world change if Black humanity was recognized? If we centered the marginalized in our movements? When you use your imagination, it'll help you approach your conversations with children with an open heart and mind. Otherwise, you may find yourself thinking, "But that wouldn't work in the real world," rather than focusing on the possibilities and being fully present with your young person.

Remember, systems are made and put into place by people. That means that new systems can be made and put into place by other people. As Ursula K. Le Guin said, "We live in capitalism, its power seems inescapable—but then, so did the divine right of kings. Any human power can be resisted and changed by human beings." This can feel like hard work, and it's an ongoing journey. But if we do this work, all of us together, then we can offer our children a world to live in that is better and more just than the one they were born into. Thank you for embarking on this journey with me.

With gratitude,

Jalena

BLACK LIVES MATTER

#BlackLivesMatter was founded in 2013 in response to the acquittal of Trayvon Martin's murderer. Black Lives Matter Global Network Foundation, Inc. is a global organization in the US, UK, and Canada, whose mission is to eradicate white supremacy and build local power to intervene in violence inflicted on Black communities by the state and vigilantes. By combating and countering acts of violence, creating space for Black imagination and innovation, and centering Black joy, we are winning immediate improvements in our lives.

We are expansive. We are a collective of liberators who believe in an inclusive and spacious movement. We also believe that in order to win and bring as many people with us along the way, we must move beyond the narrow nationalism that is all too prevalent in Black communities. We must ensure we are building a movement that brings all of us to the front.

We affirm the lives of Black queer and trans folks, disabled folks, undocumented folks, folks with records, women, and all Black lives along the gender spectrum. Our network centers those who have been marginalized within Black liberation movements.

We are working for a world where Black lives are no longer systematically targeted for demise.

We affirm our humanity, our contributions to this society, and our resilience in the face of deadly oppression.

The call for Black lives to matter is a rallying cry for ALL Black lives striving for liberation.